RULES FOR YOUTH SOCCER

Keith A. Kurtz

An easy version of the Laws of the Game with advice
2023-24 Edition

© Copyright 2023 Keith A. Kurtz
All rights reserved.

The information in this book was correct at the time of publication, but the Author does not assume any liability for loss or damage caused by errors or omissions.

Ebook: 979-8-9865754-2-1
Paperback: 979-8-9865754-3-8

FORWARD

This book has a twofold purpose: (1) to be used in conjunction with an introductory referee training course and (2) to be used as a manual for referees who are primarily assigned games in the Under-12 and younger divisions.

I carried two awesome books in my soccer bag when I was a new referee: *Fair or Foul* by Paul and Larry Harris and *The Rules of Soccer: Simplified* by Bill Mason and Larry Maisner. These books are my inspiration and served me well. I want every referee to have something similar to tuck into their bag for the odd moment when a question pops up.

The Laws of the Game are presented in a concise and easy-to-read format with bits of advice interspersed. The laws are not presented in their entirety. Rather, I have attempted to address the parts of each law that are needed for ages 12 and younger. It is a work in progress and your suggestions are welcome. Please send your ideas to ayso174rdri@gmail.com.

I hope that this book serves you well and look forward to seeing you on the pitch someday!

Keith A. Kurtz

Rules for Youth Soccer is available as a Kindle E-book. Please see keithkurtz.net/soccer for details.

LAW 1
The Field of Play

The field of play (pitch) with dimensions

Soccer fields vary in size. Fields intended for youth play are often smaller than the dimensions shown with the penalty area, goal area, and center circle scaled down proportionally. Regardless, a soccer field must be longer that it is wide.

Most leagues require goal nets. Goals must be anchored securely to the ground for safety. If the field is marked with multiple colors, ensure that coaches and players know which lines are being used before the match begins.

Flags at each corner are required with a minimum height of 5 feet (for safety). There may be flags at the half-way line and must be at least 3 feet outside the touch line.

Learn the correct names and dimensions. Referring to the parts of the field by their correct names will reflect on your professionalism and reassure people that you know what you are doing and can be trusted.

What should you do if the field does not meet all these conditions even after all reasonable efforts have been made? With two exceptions, find a way to play the game!

The two exceptions are safety related:

- The goals **must** be securely anchored so that they will not tip over and potentially cause injury during the match.
- Holes in the field where a player or referee may injure themselves **must** be made safe. Dangerous objects on or near the field that may cause injury should be removed.

Your primary responsibility is safety and you must not start a match when either of these conditions is present.

Terminology is important. The lines along the short side of the field are *goal lines* and stretch corner to corner. The line across the center of the field is the *half-way line*. The large rectangle in front of each goal is the *penalty area*. The small rectangle in front of each goal is the *goal area*.

The lines along the long side of the field are the *touch lines,* **not** the sidelines. The name "touch line" came into being during the early years of the modern game of soccer. When the ball leaves the field, a player is allowed to pick up the ball with their hands. That is, they may touch the ball with their hands when the ball is "in touch" (off the field).

Note that the outside edge of the lines surrounding an area are the area boundary. That is, lines are part of the area they enclose.

LAW 2
The Ball

The ball must be spherical and made of suitable material.

A standard No. 5 ball, used in 14U and older, is 27-28 inches in circumference and weighs between 14-16 ounces. 10U and 12U typically use a No. 4 ball. 8U and younger typically use a No. 3 ball. Specifications for the smaller balls are less exact. If the ball is marked No. 3 or No. 4, you should trust that it is a No. 3 or No. 4

The ball should not be badly out-of-round or have large pieces of the outer cover missing.

Additional balls may be placed near (not in) the goals to be used as spares. The referee should inspect all balls to be used in the match.

The ball pressure should be approximately one atmosphere above ambient (IFAB specifies 8.5-15.6 psi above atmospheric pressure at sea level). This is not as difficult to determine as it may sound. Simply hold the ball with both hands and press firmly into the ball with both thumbs together. A properly inflated ball will depress one-quarter to one-half inch. It will not take you more than a couple of games before you have a good sense of what a properly inflated ball feels like.

If nobody has the correct size ball, play the game with the ball that you have. It is safe, fair, and a lot more fun than not playing!

LAW 3
The Players

A team may have no more than 11 players on the field, one of whom must be the goalkeeper. For 11-a-side soccer (11 players on each team), the game may not start unless each team has at least 7 players.

Many youth leagues encourage short-sided games for younger divisions, especially 12U and younger. This is to encourage player participation and development. You will need to find out the exact number of players for each age group from your local administrators. Many youth leagues specify a minimum amount of time that each player is required to play.

For example, AYSO encourages regions to play 9-a-side in 12U and 7-a-side in 10U. In 8U and younger, there may not be goalkeepers and the number of players on a side may vary from season to season. AYSO requires that each player play for at least half of the game unless they arrive late. Many AYSO regions require that each player play for at least three-quarters of each game and specify a maximum amount of time that a player may be the goalkeeper in the younger divisions.

Substitutions may occur only during a game stoppage. The referee must be informed who then allows the substitution. It is important to keep track of who the players and who the substitutes are. You should always be aware of the number of players on the field. Players should enter the field at the half-way line with one player exiting the field before the new player enters. This can be difficult to manage. Do the best that you can while keeping the game fun.

If you discover that one team has too many players on the field and the ball is not in play, notify the team's bench and let the coach handle it.

If the ball is in play, you should stop play and notify the team's bench. In an older match, the player that is brought off the field in this situation may be cautioned and shown the yellow card. Outside of the most competitive club matches, younger players should not be cautioned.

If play is stopped solely to remove an extra player, restart with indirect free kick only if a player is cautioned, otherwise restart with a dropped ball. If a goal is scored by a team with too many players on the field, the extra person affected the play, and play has not restarted, the goal is denied, and play is restarted with a goal kick or corner kick depending on who last touched the ball. If play was restarted prior to discovery of the extra player, the goal stands.

Any player may change places with the goalkeeper if:

- The referee is informed before the change is made.
- The change is made during a stoppage in play.

Should a player change place with the goalkeeper without the referees permission:

Allow play to continue.

- Instruct younger players that the change was done incorrectly when the ball is next out or play, but not if the change occurred during half-time, half-time of extra time, immediately before extra time, or before kicks from the penalty mark.
- In older age groups (14U and older) both players should be cautioned with the exceptions noted above.

LAW 4
The Players' Equipment

Inspect players' and substitutes' equipment prior to the match. Ensure that players are not wearing anything that may be dangerous to themselves or others. Political, religious, or personal statements or slogans are not allowed. Jewelry is not allowed and may not be covered with tape. Medical alert bracelets must be safely covered in such a way that medical personal can see the alert bracelet and read what it says.

Some competitions have strict requirements regarding uniforms and undergarments, and these must be followed. For most recreational youth competitions, be reasonable and find a way to permit a player to play with a less than perfect uniform.

The guidelines for uniforms are not complicated:

- The two teams' jerseys must be of different colors.
- Players must wear shorts, a separate shirt or jersey, socks, shin guards, and shoes.
- Goalkeepers may wear track suit bottoms and/or hats without a stiff brim
- Shin guards must be underneath and completely covered by the socks. Do not allow players to fold their socks down over the shin guards. They must be underneath the sock.
- Goalkeeper shirt colors should be different from each other, from the two team jersey colors, and from the official's shirt color. Be easy on this point. Many teams only have one goalkeeper shirt. If the goalkeeper's shirt is the same or similar color as either team's jersey, consider having them wear a pinnie to avoid confusion.

LAW 5
The Referee

Each match is controlled by a referee who has full authority to enforce the Laws of the Game in connection with the match.

As the referee, you are responsible for ensuring that the match is safe, fair, and fun. You should do your best to make the match enjoyable for the players, coaches, spectators, you, and your fellow officials.

In addition to enforcing the Laws of the Game, you are responsible for these basic duties:

- Act as timekeeper and keep a record of the match, including the game score.
- Manage substitutions along with the assistant referees.
- Submit a match report to the appropriate authority following the match.
- Stop play when a player is or may be injured or ill.
- Restart play after it has been stopped.

Along with enforcing the Laws of the Game (LOTG), the referee is expected to contribute to the Spirit of the Game (SOTG). A past International Board Decision (IBD) captures this concept:

> The Laws of the Game are intended to provide that games should be played with as little interference as possible, and in this view, it is the duty of referees to penalize only deliberate breaches of the Law. Constant whistling for trifling and doubtful breaches produces bad feeling and loss of temper on the part of the players and spoils the pleasure of spectators.

LAW 6
The Other Match Officials

The two assistant referees assist the referee in controlling the match. Assistant referees advise the referee who makes all match decisions. Sometimes the referee chooses to not accept the referee's advice and will use a prearranged signal to indicate this. In all circumstances, assistant referees must support the referee and his or her decisions.

Assistant referees signal:

- When the ball passes out of bounds and which team is entitled to the throw-in, goal kick, corner kick, or if a goal has been scored.
- Offside.
- When a team is requesting a substitution.
- A foul or misconduct out of view of the referee and which team is entitled to the free kick.
- When the goalkeeper has moved off the goal line prior to the ball being kicked during the taking of a penalty kick.
- For any other duties assigned by the referee in the pre-game conference.

CLUB LINESMEN

Should assistant referees not be assigned to the match, the referee may, at his or her discretion, ask that a non-neutral volunteer to assist. These non-neutral assistants are known as club linesmen. Club linesmen are asked to signal only that the ball has passed out of bounds, leaving the final decision and the direction of the restart to the referee.

LAW 7
Duration of the Match

A soccer match consists of two equal time periods. The Laws of the Game specify that each half shall last 45 minutes, but most youth leagues play shorter halves.

Typical Youth Match Durations

18U	45-minute halves	12U	30-minute halves
16U	40-minute halves	10U	25-minute halves
14U	35-minute halves	8U	20-minute halves

The referee is responsible for keeping time. The assistant referees should also keep track of time to back up the referee.

- Time starts when the ball has been put into play; it has been kicked and moves.
- Time is added at the end of each half to allow for time lost due to substitution, injury, interference by an outside agent, or other cause. The referee determines the amount of time to be added.
- Should time expire during the taking of a penalty kick, time shall be extended to allow the penalty kick to complete.
- The interval between halves is typically 5 – 10 minutes and should not exceed 15 minutes.

LAW 8
The Start and Restart of Play

A kick-off starts both halves, both halves of extra time, and after a goal is scored. Free kicks, penalty kicks, throw-ins, goal kicks, and corner kicks are addressed in other laws. A dropped ball starts play when no other restart is indicated.

If an offence occurs when the ball is not in play, it does not change the restart.

KICK-OFF

- Conduct a coin toss before the match and before the start of extra time. The referee should toss the coin after designating a player, any player, to "call it in the air."
- The winner of the coin toss may choose which goal to attack or to kick-off in the first half.
- If the coin toss winner chooses which goal to attack, the other team kicks-off in the first half.
- If the coin toss winner chooses to kick-off, the other team chooses which goal to attack.
- The kick-off always occurs at the center mark.
- All players must be on their own side of the field until the ball is put into play except for the player kicking the ball into play.
- All defenders must be outside of the center circle (10 yards) until the ball is put into play.
- The ball must be stationary prior to being put into play
- The referee must signal (blow your whistle) before the ball may be put into play.
- The ball is in play when it is kicked in any direction.

- Teams will change ends for the second half and the team that did not kick-off in the first half kicks-off in the second half.
- After a team scores a goal, the kick-off is taken by their opponents.
- The kicker may not touch the ball again after kicking-off until another player has touched the ball. Should this occur, an indirect free kick is awarded unless the kicker handles the ball, in which case a direct free kick is awarded.
- If anyone crosses the halfway line or the defense enters the center circle before the ball is put into play, the kick-off is retaken.
- A goal may be scored directly from a kick-off, but only against the kicking team's opponents. If the ball enters the kicker's goal, restart with a corner kick.

DROPPED BALL

A dropped ball is used to restart play for an unusual but neutral reason such as an injury, a dog on the field, or a stray ball on the field that may interfere with play.

- Drop the ball where it was last touched by a player, an outside agent, or a match official (see Law 9 for this).
- Drop the ball from the player's waist height (not your waist height!).
- The ball is in play when it touches the ground.
- The ball is dropped in front of a player from the team that had possession when play was stopped unless play was stopped in the penalty area.
- If play was stopped in the penalty area, the ball is dropped in front of the goalkeeper.
- All other players, from both teams, must remain at least 4.5 yards from the ball until it is in play.
- If a player touches the ball before it touches the ground, the ball is dropped again.
- A goal may not be scored until a second player touches the ball.

LAW 9
The Ball In and Out of Play

The ball is out of play when it has passed completely over the outside edge of the goal line or touch line, either on the ground or in the air. The ball is also out of play when play has been stopped by the referee.

Should the ball touch the referee, or an assistant referee, the ball remains in play unless:

- a team starts a promising attack.
- the ball goes directly into a goal.
- the team in possession of the ball changes.

In all these cases, restart with a dropped ball.

The ball remains in play when it rebounds off a goal post, crossbar, or corner flag and remains on the field of play.

You do not usually need to blow your whistle when the ball goes out of play if it is obvious to everyone. Blow your whistle if players continue to play the ball and use your voice. Say something like "That one went out! The throw-in is back here."

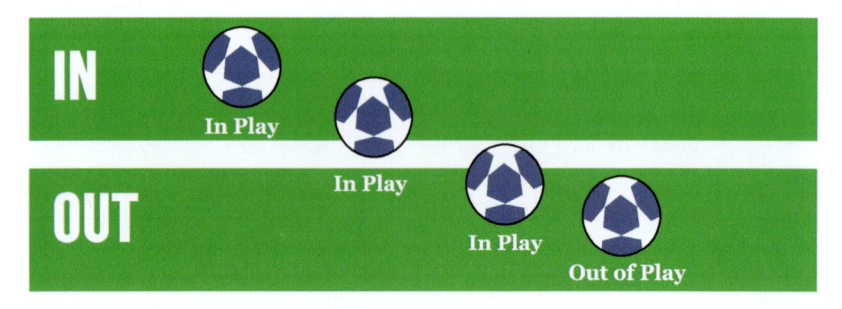

LAW 10
Determining the Outcome of a Match

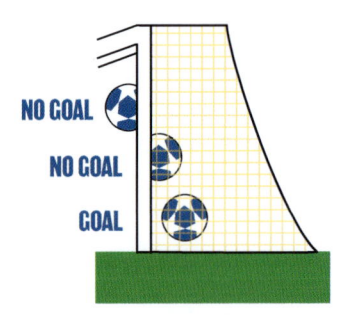

NO GOAL
NO GOAL
GOAL

A goal is scored when all of the ball passes completely over the outside edge of the goal line, between the goal posts, under the crossbar, and the ball is in play. Any player may score a goal for either team, including the goalkeeper.

Soccer is a difficult game in which to score and there are often controversies surrounding the referee's decision to award a goal. For this reason, it is important for the assistant referees to follow the ball all the way to the goal line to accurately judge whether the ball has passed completely over the goal line.

A player may score a goal against their own team. This is referred to as an "own goal."

If the goalkeeper throws the ball directly into the opponent's goal, a goal is not awarded, and play is restarted with a goal kick.

A goal may not be scored directly from a throw-in.

A goal may be scored directly from a goal kick or corner kick, but only against the opposing team.

Signal that a goal has been scored by pointing towards the center circle. You should not blow your whistle unless the ball has come back onto the field and players continue to play it. The assistant referee signals a fair goal by moving quickly towards the halfway line with the flag at their side.

DRAWN MATCH

In the case where no goals are scored or each team scores an equal number of goals, the match is drawn (results in a tie). Drawn matches are normally allowed to stand.

In some competitions, a winner must be determined. In these cases, the rules of the competition will dictate how a drawn match is resolved. The most common, but by no means only, method of "breaking a tie" is to play two equal periods of extra time. Should extra time not result in a winner, the game progresses to penalties. The rules of the competition will specify the length of time for each period of extra time.

Should penalties be part of the tie breaking formula, be sure to remind both coaches that only players in the game at the end of extra time will be allowed to participate. You and the assistant referees should make note of who is playing in the second period of extra time.

LAW 11
Offside

When the modern game of Association Football (Soccer) was developed in the English public schools, it was considered unfair for a player to run off their side (team), past the defenders, and wait by themselves for an opportunity to score. This philosophy is codified in Law 11 which is intended to force the side to work together to advance the ball and score.

For an offside offence to occur, an attacking player must be in offside position and be involved in active play. The restart is an indirect free kick for the opposing team.

Offside Position

A player is in offside position if he or she:

- is in the opponents' half of the field.
- is closer to the opponents' goal line than the second-to-last defender.
- is closer to the opponents' goal line than the ball.

Active Play

Most of us have an intuitive sense of what "active play" means, but there are some less than obvious situations.

A player is involved in active play by:

- interfering with play by playing or touching a ball passed or touched by a team-mate or
- interfering with an opponent by:
    - preventing an opponent from playing or being able to play the ball by clearly obstructing the opponent's line of vision or

- challenging an opponent for the ball or
- clearly attempting to play a ball which is close when this action impacts on an opponent or
- making an obvious action which clearly impacts on the ability of an opponent to play the ball

or

- gaining an advantage by playing the ball or interfering with an opponent when it has:
  - rebounded or been deflected off the goalpost, crossbar, match official or an opponent
  - been deliberately saved by any opponent.

Moment of Judgment

A player may only be guilty of committing an offside offence if they are *in offside position at the moment a teammate plays or touches the ball.*

Not Offside

A player is never offside when he or she:

- receives the ball directly from a throw-in, corner kick, or goal kick.
- receives the ball directly from an opponent.

Referee Dynamics

Judging potential offside offences is an important duty of the assistant referees (AR). Each AR must be diligent in aligning themselves with the second-to-last defender. The exception is when the defenders all move into their opponents' half of the field when the AR shall stand even with the half-way line.

If you find yourself without ARs and practicing the so-called "one-man system," you will need to run down the field during every attack to put yourself in a position to accurately judge offside position.

LAW 11 | Offside

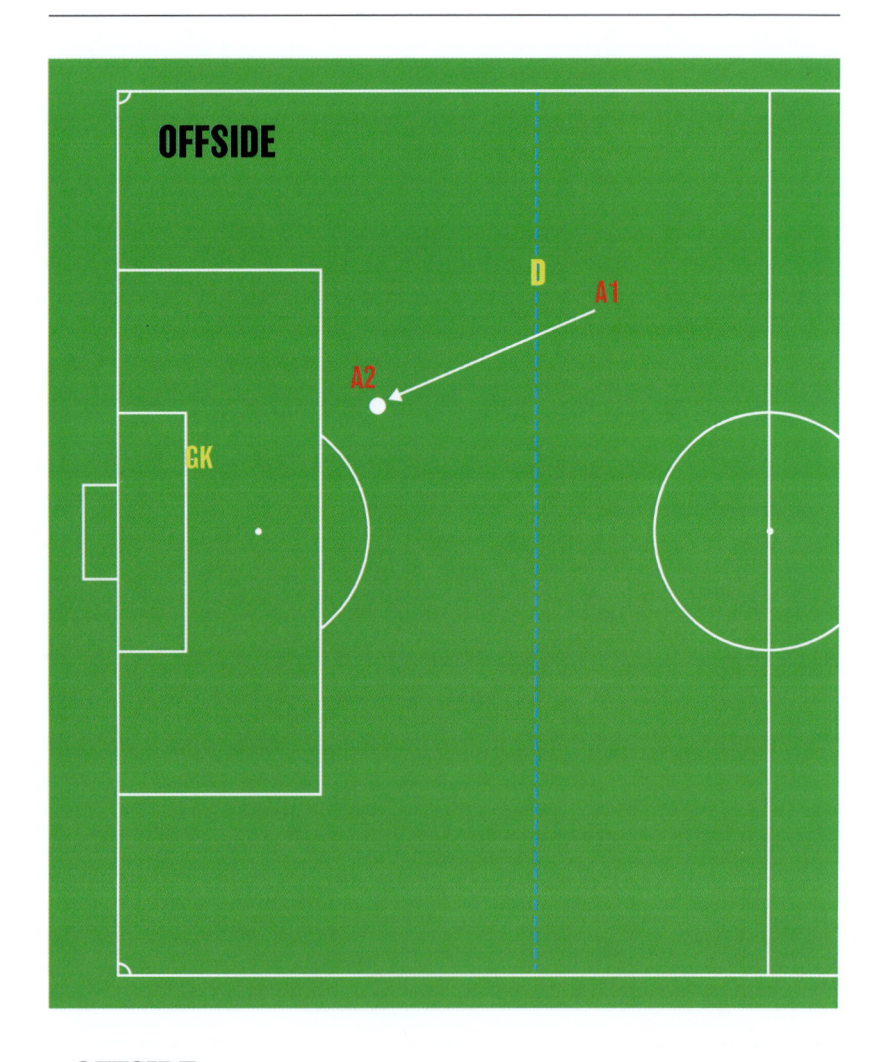

OFFSIDE

Attacker A1 has passed the ball to A2. At the moment the ball is passed, A2 is in an offside position because there is only one defender, the goalkeeper, between A2 and the goal.

20

LAW 11 | Offside

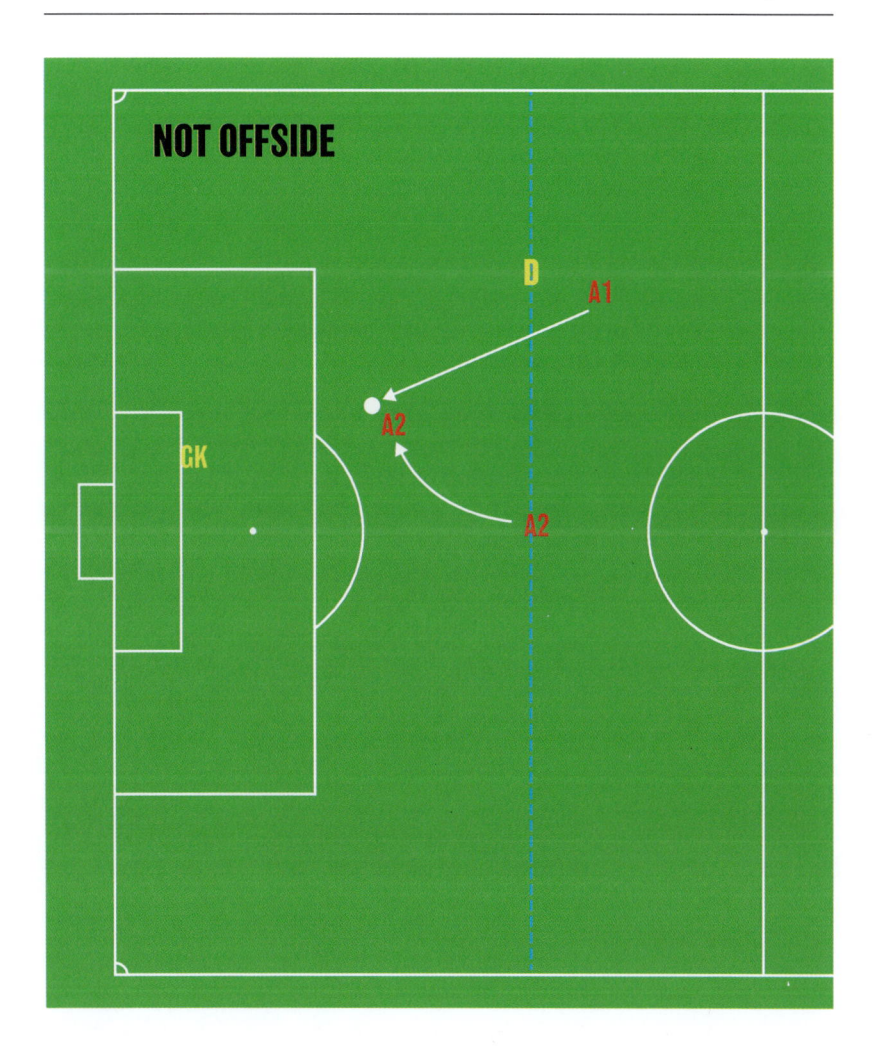

NOT OFFSIDE

Attacker A1 has passed the ball to A2. At the moment the ball is passed, A2 is not in an offside position because he or she is even with or behind the second to last defender, D. It does not matter where A2 collects the ball provided he or she is not in offside position when the ball is passed by a teammate.

LAW 11 | Offside

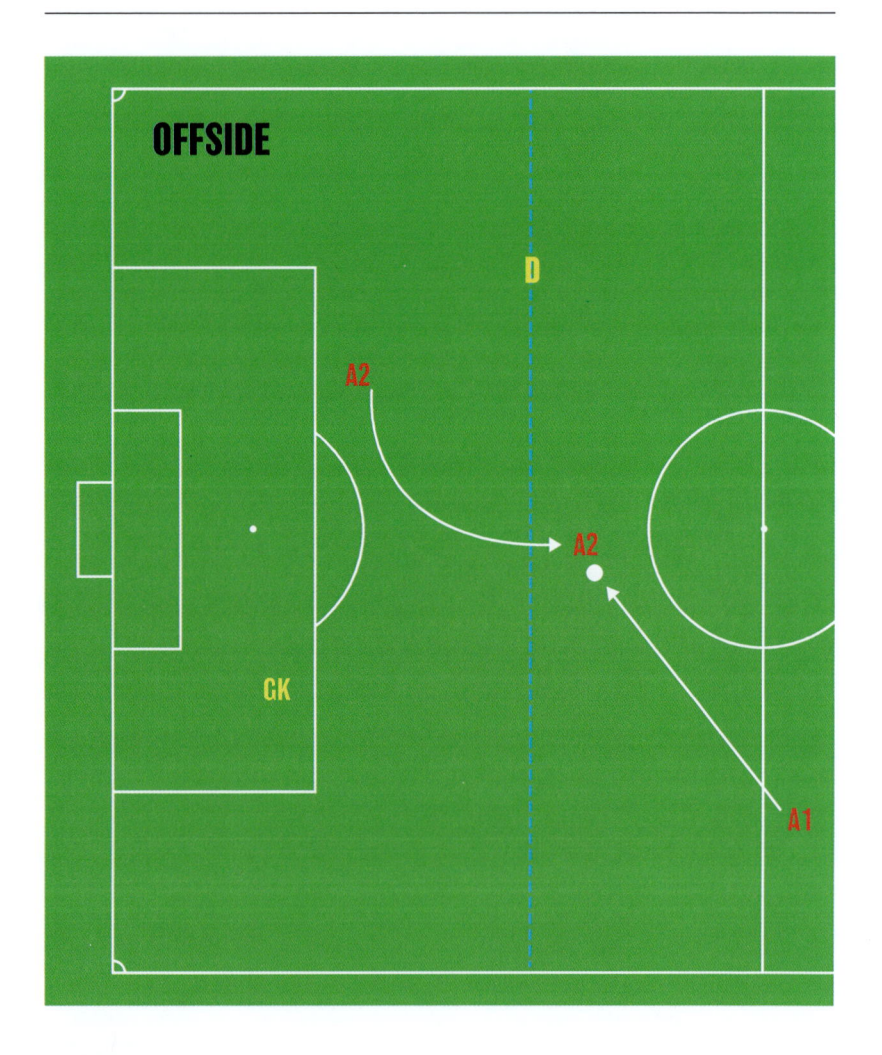

OFFSIDE

Attacker A1 has passed the ball to A2. At the moment the ball is passed, A2 is in an offside position because there is only one defender, the goalkeeper, between A2 and the goal. The fact that A2 ran back onside to collect the ball does not matter. A2 was in offside position at the moment the ball was played by a teammate.

LAW 12
Fouls and Misconduct

There are two types of fouls:

- Fouls that result in a direct free kick
- Fouls that result in an indirect free kick

Direct Free Kick Fouls

The following offences result in a direct free kick if they are considered by the referee to be careless, reckless, or using excessive force:

- Charges an opponent
- Jumps at an opponent
- Kicks or attempts to kick an opponent
- Pushes an opponent
- Strikes or attempts to strike an opponent
- Tackles or challenges an opponent
- Trips or attempts to trip an opponent

The following offences result in a direct free kick:

- A handball offence (except for the goalkeeper in their own penalty area)
- Holds an opponent
- Impedes an opponent with contact
- Bites or spits at someone on the team lists or a match official.
- Throws an object at the ball, an opponent, or match official, or makes contact with the ball with a held object.

Handling the Ball

It is a handball offence if a player:

- deliberately touches the ball with their hand/arm.
- gains possession/control of the ball after it has touched their hand/arm and then:
  - scores in the opponents' goal.
  - creates a goal-scoring opportunity.
- scores in the opponents' goal directly from their hand/arm, even if accidental.

It is okay to play the ball from the shoulder. The boundary between the shoulder and the arm is defined as the bottom of the armpit.

There are situations where the ball may touch a player's hand/arm that are not considered a handball offence. Unless a player has made their body unnaturally larger by extending their arms or extended their arms over their shoulder level, a ball striking a player's hand or arm is not a handball offence except in the above circumstances. A good rule of thumb is to consider whether the ball touched the player, or the player touched the ball.

Indirect Free Kick Fouls

An indirect free kick is awarded if a player:

- plays in a dangerous manner.
- impedes the progress of an opponent without contact.
- is guilty of dissent, using offensive, insulting or abusive language, and/or gestures or other verbal offences
- prevents the goalkeeper from releasing the ball.
- commits any other offence where play has been stopped to administer a caution or send-off.

An indirect free kick is awarded if a goalkeeper, inside their own penalty area:

- controls the ball with the hand/arm for more than six seconds before releasing it. Please do your best to not call this offence. If a young goalkeeper is taking too much time, you should instruct them to put the ball in play.
- touches the ball with the hand/arm after releasing it and before it has touched another player.
- touches the ball with the hand/arm after it has been *deliberately* kicked to the goalkeeper by a teammate.
- touches the ball with the hand/arm after receiving it directly from a throw-in taken by a teammate.

Discipline

Law 12 lists the situations in which a player may be cautioned (yellow card) or sent-off (red card). There are so few situations in which using cards with younger players is appropriate, they are not mentioned here. If you see behavior developing that must be stopped, the best course of action is to ask the player to stop. If that does not work, talk to the coach so that the two of you can work together to teach the player appropriate behavior.

LAW 13
Free Kicks

There are two types of free kicks, direct and indirect. Law 12 describes the fouls that are associated with each type. An indirect free kick is also awarded for an offside offence or a "second touch."

Direct Free Kick

A goal may be scored for the kicking team by *directly* kicking the ball into the opponent's goal.

Indirect Free Kick

A goal may only be scored for the kicking team if the ball touches another player, from either team, before entering the goal. The referee signals an indirect free kick by putting one arm straight up and holding it until the ball is touched by another player or it goes out of bounds.

Procedure

- The ball must be stationary when it is kicked.
- Free kicks are taken from where the offence occurred, with the following exceptions:
    - A free kick taken by the defense inside its own goal area may be taken from anywhere in the goal area.
    - A free kick taken by the attacking team inside its opponent's goal area is taken from the nearest point on the goal area line which runs parallel to the goal line. Defenders must be 10 yards from the ball or on the goal line between the goal posts.

LAW 13 | Free Kicks

- The ball is in play after it has been touched and clearly moves.
- Defenders must remain 10 yards from the ball in all directions until the ball is in play except as noted above. The kicking team does not have to wait for the defenders to move back.
- Defenders must remain outside of the penalty area for kicks taken within the kicking team's penalty area until the ball is in play.
- If the ball is kicked *directly* into the kicking team's goal, restart with a corner kick. If anyone touches the ball before it goes into the goal, that's a goal!
- The kicker may not touch the ball a second time until another player touches the ball. Restart with an indirect free kick.
- If the defense forms a wall with 3 or more players, members of the attacking team must remain 1 yard from the wall until the ball is in play.
- Do not allow players to delay the taking of a free kick by standing or walking in front of the ball.

LAW 14
Penalty Kicks

A penalty kick is awarded when a player commits a direct free kick foul inside their own penalty area. A goal may be scored directly from a penalty kick. Signal a penalty kick by pointing to the penalty mark. The smart referee will run towards the penalty mark while blowing their whistle and signaling. This helps to "sell the call."

Procedure

- Pick up the ball, hand it to the kicker, and instruct them to place it on the penalty mark.
- The defending goalkeeper must have at least part of one foot touching, in line with, or behind the goal line when the ball is kicked. They must be between the goalposts and not touching any part of the goal.
- All other players must remain outside of the penalty area, penalty arc, and behind the ball.
- Ask the goalkeeper if they are ready.
- After the goalkeeper confirms they are ready, blow your whistle for the kick to be taken. If the kicker plays the ball before you signal, retake the kick.
- The ball must move forward when it is kicked.
- The ball is in play when it is kicked and clearly moves.
- The kicker may not touch the ball a second time until another player touches the ball. Restart with an indirect free kick.

LAW 14 | Penalty Kicks

Encroachment and Goalkeeper Moving Early

If you do not remember all of these things, go with what is most fair and you will almost always get it right!

- If the goalkeeper "comes off their line" early and the ball goes into the goal, the goal stands.
- If the goalkeeper "comes off their line" early and the ball does not go into the goal, retake the kick.
  - An exception to this rule is the case where the kick misses the goal or rebounds from the goal (without a touch from the goalkeeper) unless the offence clearly affected the kicker. In this situation, the goalkeeper's offence is not penalized, and play continues.
- If the defending team runs into the penalty area or across the penalty arc early and the ball goes into the goal, the goal stands.
- If the defending team runs into the penalty area or across the penalty arc early and the ball does not go into the goal, retake the kick.
- If the kicking team runs into the penalty area or across the penalty arc early and the ball goes into the goal, retake the kick.
- If the kicking team runs into the penalty area or across the penalty arc early and the ball does not go into the goal, stop play and restart with an Indirect Free Kick for the goalkeeper's team.
- If the kicker kicks the ball backwards, stop play and restart with an Indirect Free Kick for the goalkeeper's team.

LAW 15
The Throw-in

A throw-in is awarded to the opponents of the player who last touched the ball when the whole of the ball passes over the outside edge of the touchline, either on the ground or in the air.

Procedure

- The throw-in is taken from the point where the ball left the field of play.
- At the moment the thrower releases the ball, the thrower must:
  - stand facing the field of play.
  - have both feet on the ground. Part of each foot must be behind or touching the touch line.
  - throw the ball with both hands from behind and over the head.
- Opponents must remain 2 yards from the thrower until the ball is in play.
- The thrower may not touch the ball a second time until another player touches the ball. Restart with an indirect free kick.
- If the ball does not enter the field when thrown, retake the throw.
- If the ball enters the field, then leaves the field without being touched, the other team throws from where the ball left the field.
- If the throw is taken improperly (e.g., foot off the ground, foot completely over the touch line), the other team throws from the same spot.
- If the ball passes *directly* into a goal from a throw-in, there is no goal. The restart is a goal kick or corner kick, depending on which goal the ball entered.
- A player is never offside when they receive the ball directly from a throw-in.

LAW 16
Goal Kick

A goal kick is awarded when the whole of the ball passes over the goal line, on the ground or in the air, having last been touched by a member of the attacking team and a goal is not scored.

A goal may be scored directly from a goal kick for the kicking team. If the ball is kicked directly into the kicker's goal, restart with a corner kick.

Procedure

- The ball must be stationary and kicked from any point within the goal area by a member of the kicking team.
- A ball may be placed on the goal area boundary line or with some part of the ball within the outside edge of the boundary line.
- The ball is in play when it is kicked and clearly moves.
- Opponents must remain outside of the penalty area until the ball is in play.
- The kicker may not touch the ball a second time until another player touches the ball. Restart with an indirect free kick.
- A player is never offside when they receive the ball directly from a goal kick.

LAW 16 | Goal Kick

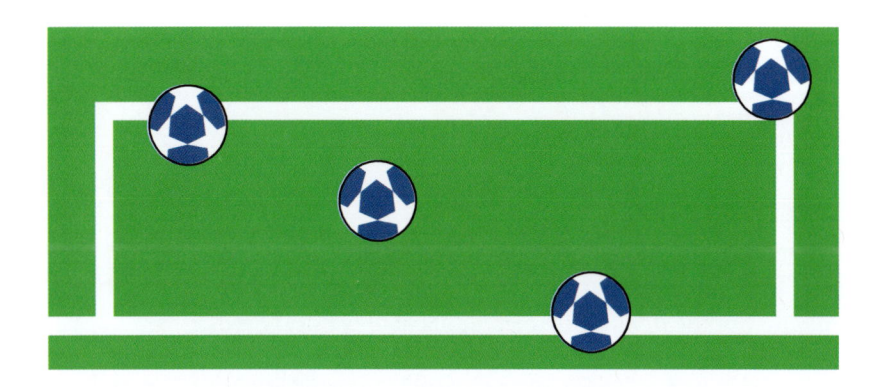

Each of these balls is placed correctly for a goal kick.

LAW 17
Corner Kick

A corner kick is awarded when the whole of the ball passes over the goal line, on the ground or in the air, having last been touched by a member of the defending team and a goal is not scored.

A goal may be scored directly from a corner kick for the kicking team. If the ball is kicked directly into the kicker's goal, restart with a corner kick.

Procedure

- The corner kick is taken from the corner arc nearest to the point where the ball went out of play.
- The ball must be stationary and kicked from any point within the corner arc by a member of the attacking team.
- A ball on the corner arc boundary line or having some part of the ball within the outside edge of the boundary line, is legally placed.
- The ball is in play when it is kicked and clearly moves.
- Opponents must remain 10 yards from the corner arc until the ball is in play.
- The corner flag may not be moved to make it easier to take a corner kick. If you see that the flag has fallen over, it is permissible to reset the flag so that it is vertical. You should do this yourself to avoid the appearance of allowing players moving the flag out of the way.
- The kicker may not touch the ball a second time until another player touches the ball. Restart with an indirect free kick.
- A player is never offside when they receive the ball directly from a corner kick.

LAW 17 | Corner Kick

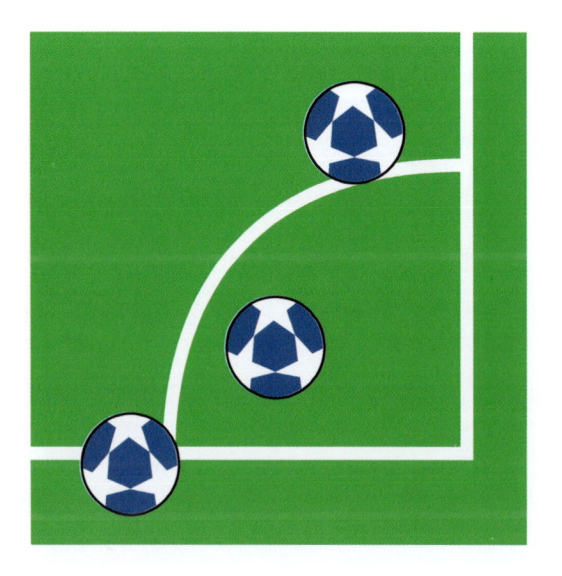

Each of these balls is placed correctly for a corner kick.

Assistant Referee Signals

Stop and face the field before making any signal.

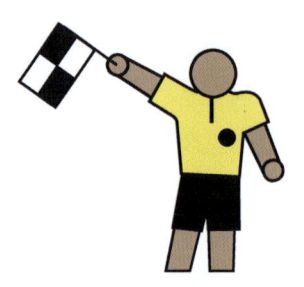

Throw-in Attacking Team
Hold flag straight up, then point in the direction the attacking team is going.

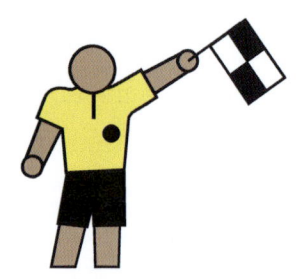

Throw-in Defending Team
Hold flag straight up, then point in the direction the defending team is going.

Substitution
Hold flag horizontally over your head and slightly forward so the flag is not *on* your head

Corner Kick (either corner)
Hold flag at a 45° angle to your right regardless of which corner will be used.

Goal Kick
Hold flag horizontal, pointing straight across the field and parallel with the goal line.

Assistant Referee Signals

Free Kick Attacking Team
Raise flag straight up, obtain eye contact with referee, shake flag a few times, point in the direction the attacking team is going after the referee blows the whistle.

Free Kick Defending Team
Raise flag straight up, obtain eye contact with referee, shake flag a few times, point in the direction the defending team is going after the referee blows the whistle.

AR Signals for Offside

To signal offside, stop and face the field, then hold the flag straight up until one of three things happens:

1. The referee stops play for offside at which time you indicate where on the field the offence occurred.

2. The referee decides to not call an offside offence and waves off your signal.

3. The offside becomes moot because the ball has gone out of bounds or the opposing team has gained control of the ball and has advanced it up the field.

If there is an offside offence and the ball is kicked into the net, hold your flag up until acknowledged by the referee.

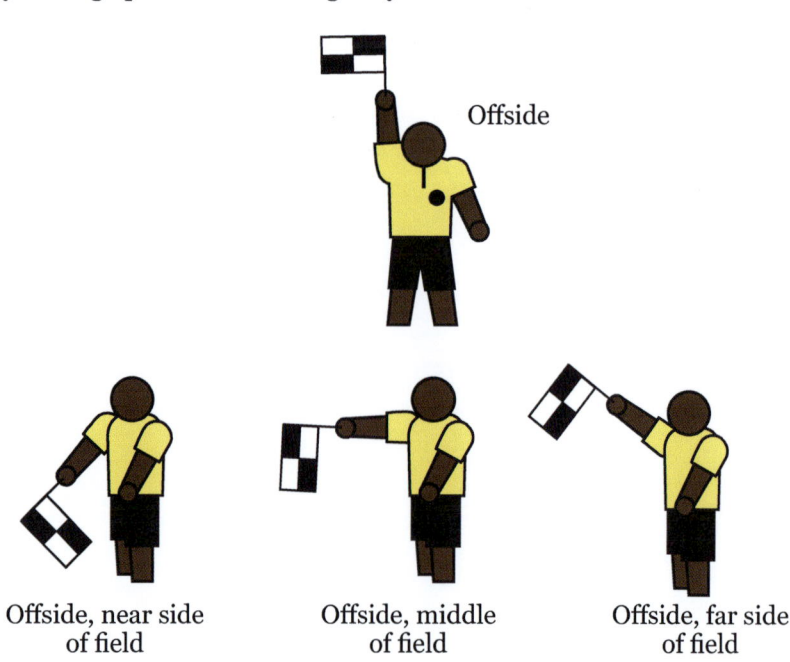

Offside

| Offside, near side of field | Offside, middle of field | Offside, far side of field |

PENALTIES

Penalties (penalty shoot-outs) are sometimes used to determine a winner in a tied game. Before penalties may start:

- The Laws of the game state that the referee shall toss a coin to decide the goal at which the kicks will be taken. In youth matches, the referee may decide on the goal in consultation with his or her assistant referees, taking conditions such as wind and sun into account. Some competitions will have a separate goal set up, away from the field, for penalties. This is done to clear the field and enable the next match to start in a timely manner.
- The referee will designate one assistant referee to be the goal judge. The goal judge will determine whether the ball has passed entirely over the goal line after being kicked, and if the goalkeeper has left the goal line prior to the ball being kicked. Be sure to pre-arrange a signal for the goal judge to indicate any situation needing your attention.
- The other assistant referee will stay in the center circle to help manage the teams and to keep track of who has taken their kick.
- Only the players in the game when time runs out, including extra time, may participate in penalties. An exception to this rule is the case where the goalkeeper is unable to continue and may be replaced by one of the ineligible players.
- The goalkeeper is an eligible kicker.
- If one team has more eligible players than the other, they must reduce their number so that the teams are equal.
- A coin toss is conducted, and the winner chooses whether their team kicks first or second.
- The referee is not informed of the kicking order. This allows teams to determine the kicking order as the kicks progress.

During penalties:

- Follow the procedure for Law 14, Penalty Kicks.
- The goalkeeper of the kicking team should remain on the goal line, outside of the penalty area, and make no motion or sound that may distract the other goalkeeper.
- Any eligible player may change places with the goalkeeper.
- Each kick is completed when the ball goes out of play or stops moving.
- The kicker may not play the ball a second time.
- The referee keeps track of the score.
- Each kick is taken by a different player, and all eligible players must take a kick before any player may take a second kick.
- Each team takes five kicks, alternately, unless one team scores more goals than the other could even if all five kicks are taken.
- If the score is tied after five kicks, kicks continue until one team has scored one more goal than the other from the same number of kicks.
- If the score is tied after all eligible players have kicked, a team may change the kicking order for additional kicks. Every eligible player must take a second kick before any may take a third, and so on.

Player Development Initiatives

The Player Development Initiatives (PDIs) are a set of standards adopted by US Soccer and apply to all youth member organizations in the United States, including state associations, U.S. Youth Soccer, U.S. Club Soccer, AYSO, SAY and others. The PDIs aim to create an environment for youth players to grow and develop their soccer abilities.

The most notable PDIs include standards for small-sided games where youth teams are composed of less than 11 members, smaller field dimensions, and smaller ball sizes.

Age Group	6U, 7U, 8U	9U, 10U	11U, 12U
Field Size (yards)	Length 25-35 Width 15-25	Length 55-65 Width 35-45	Length 70-80 Width 45-55
Max Goal Size (feet)	Height 4 Width 6	Height 6.5 Width 18.5	Height 7 Width 21
Players	4v4	7v7	9v9
Ball Size	3	4	4
Game Time (minutes)[1]	4x10	2x25	2x30
Offside	No	Yes	Yes

[1] Youth leagues may adjust game times.

There are some special rules for younger players intended to increase opportunities for players to develop and/or to promote safety.

Goalkeepers and Offside

Most youth leagues do not allow goalkeepers in U6, U7, and U8. Offside is not in effect for these age groups and should not be enforced.

Punts and Drop Kicks

Goalkeepers in 9U and 10U may not drop kick or punt the ball. If a goalkeeper punts or drop kicks the ball, award an indirect free kick to the opposing team from the spot of the offense. If the punt or drop kick occurs within the goal area, the indirect free kick should be taken on the goal area line parallel to the goal line at the nearest point to where the infringement occurred.

Heading the Ball

The safety restrictions on heading the ball are not technically part of the PDIs but are included here for completeness. These restrictions have been adopted by most youth leagues in the United States, including US Youth Soccer and AYSO.

Players age 10 years of age and under may not head the ball directly from the air in any match or competition. Heading the ball in practice is also not allowed. If a player age 10 or younger **deliberately** heads the ball in a match, you should award an indirect free kick to the opposing team at the spot of the infraction. If the heading occurs within the penalty area, you should have the ball moved outside the penalty area for the indirect free kick.

Players age 11 and age 12 may head the ball in any match or competition. Coaches are expected to ensure that no player heads the ball more than 25 times per week, regardless of setting.

AYSO does not allow players to head the ball in divisions 12U and below unless there is an 11U division, in which case the restriction does not apply to 12U.

Players age 13 and older may head the ball in any match or competition and these players may practice heading the ball in an organized team practice or skill session.

The Build Out Line

The Build Out Line (BOL) is required in 9U and 10U and promotes playing the ball out of the back in a less pressured setting. Build Out Lines should be equidistant between the penalty area line and the halfway line. In the absence of a line, a BOL can be marked with training disks or cones in a way that does not endanger the players or referee. The BOL is usually marked with a different color than the other lines on the pitch.

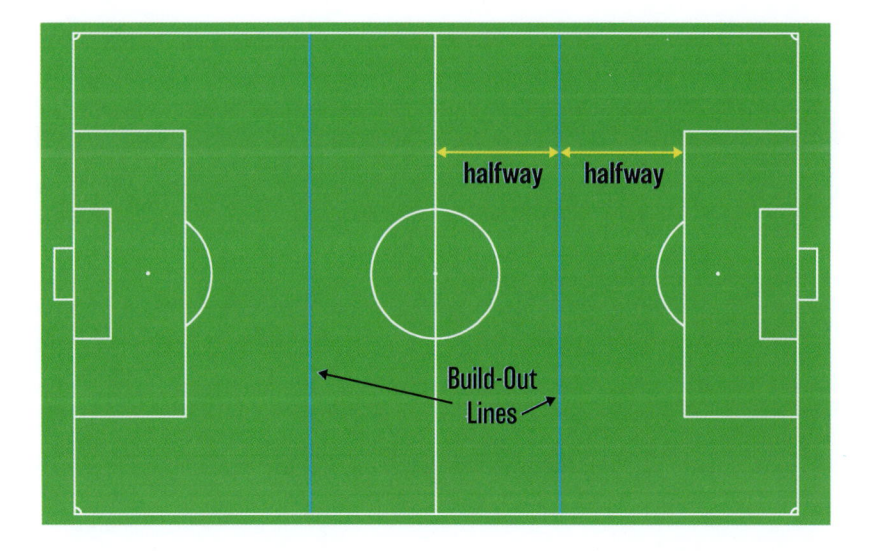

When the goalkeeper has the ball in his or her hands, the opposing team must move behind the BOL until the ball is put into play. Once the opposing team is behind the build out line, the goalkeeper may pass, throw, or roll the ball into play. After the ball is put into play by the goalkeeper, the opposing team may cross the build out line and play resumes as normal. The opposing team must also move behind the BOL prior to a goal kick and may only cross the BOL once the ball has left the penalty area.

Most goalkeepers will wait for the opponents to move behind the BOL and the "six second rule" is not in effect until they do (try to be lenient in this). The goalkeeper is not required to wait until the opponents have all moved behind the BOL and may put the ball into play sooner. As a referee, you should be alert to players forgetting to move behind the BOL or intentionally delaying the game by moving slowly. In such cases, you should encourage the players, with your voice, to move more quickly.

The BOL replaces the halfway line in the opponents' half of the field for purposes of judging offside. That is, a player may not be in offside position until they have crossed BOL in the opponents' half of the field. The allows the attacking team more room to develop an attack.

Printed in Great Britain
by Amazon